a Good Planet is hard to find.

CARTOONS BY JOHN HEINE

MENASHA RIDGE PRESS

BIRMINGHAM, ALABAMA

COPYRIGHT © 1991 BY JOHN HEINE
ALL RIGHTS RESERVED
PRINTED IN THE U.S.A.
PUBLISHED BY MENASHA RIDGE PRESS
BIRMINGHAM, ALABAMA
FIRST EDITION, FIRST PRINTING
LIBRARY OF CONGRESS CATALOGING-IN-PUBLICATION DATA

HEINE, JOHN 1950-
A good planet is hard to find/drawings by John Heine
P.   CM.

0-89732-108-1

1.HUMAN ecology-- caricatures & cartoons. 2.American
wit and humor, Pictorial. I. Title.
NC 1429.H377A4   1991
741.5'973 -- dc 20   91-14106
                                                   CIP

THIS BOOK IS DEDICATED TO MY GRANDPARENTS DONALD & GLADYS BAILEY.

A PLENTI-HOT
PRODUCTION

MANY thanks to DANNY & DENISE SAXON, ARNOLD & YAZMINE ASKEW, JOSEPH HOWARD, NATALIE & HALIM THOMPSON, WADE GILBREATH, ROB PATE, MARLA, ANN GRAY AND MY BROTHER DON FOR THEIR SUPPORT & ENCOURAGEMENT. MANY, MANY THANKS TO PATRICA BOSSART WHITAKER FOR GIVING ME A CHANCE WITH THIS BOOK. ALSO TO MIKE JONES & BOB SEHLINGER FOR POINTING ME TOWARDS MENASHA RIDGE PRESS, AND TO THEIR PRODUCTION STAFF...JESSICA...KATE + KEVIN...EARTH IS ONE OF MAN'S CORE ISSUES...

EVEN THE ARMY COULDN'T STOP THE SLOW BUT INSIDIOUS CREEPING OF MURRAY'S TIRE DUMP.
IT'S NO USE SIR!.. EVERYTHING WE SHOOT JUST BOUNCES RIGHT OFF'EM!
GAS+
SNACKZ

"Pardon us for staring, but we thought you were extinct."

"That's the genius of the damn thing senator. You can drop it from a B-1 . . .
convert it into a cruise missile or just program it to watch your parking space."

bob's bolo bomb

FROM the cherch oF SelF-APPOiNTeD PROPHETS..
the **Rev. Jack VAN Impe** describes "The **End** of the *World.*"

HEINE

Oh SAY what do U see?
I see A FREAK'N FORTUNE TO BE MADE IN LUMBER PAPER & COAL.
I SEE Like A VAST EMPTY WASTE LAND. SOME-BODY OUGHTA BUILD A SIX FLAGS OR DISNEYLAND OR SOMETHING.
I see A PIECE OF GOD'S COUNTRY IF EVER There WAS ONE. THIS Should be PRE-SERVED FOR OUR Children's SAKE.

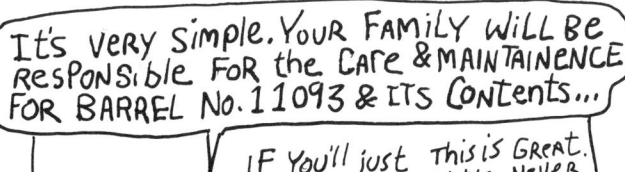

HEINE

"It's a relationship based on mutual needs. We give him water and free reign of the yard and in return he rids us of any itsy-bitsy, ucky-yucky, creepy crawlies."

"Great! Wouldn't you know it.
We finally make it to the beach and there's no room to lay out."

THE BONE

"He thinks he's really something. In a hundred million years
he'll be just another gallon of gas going into some stud's sports car."

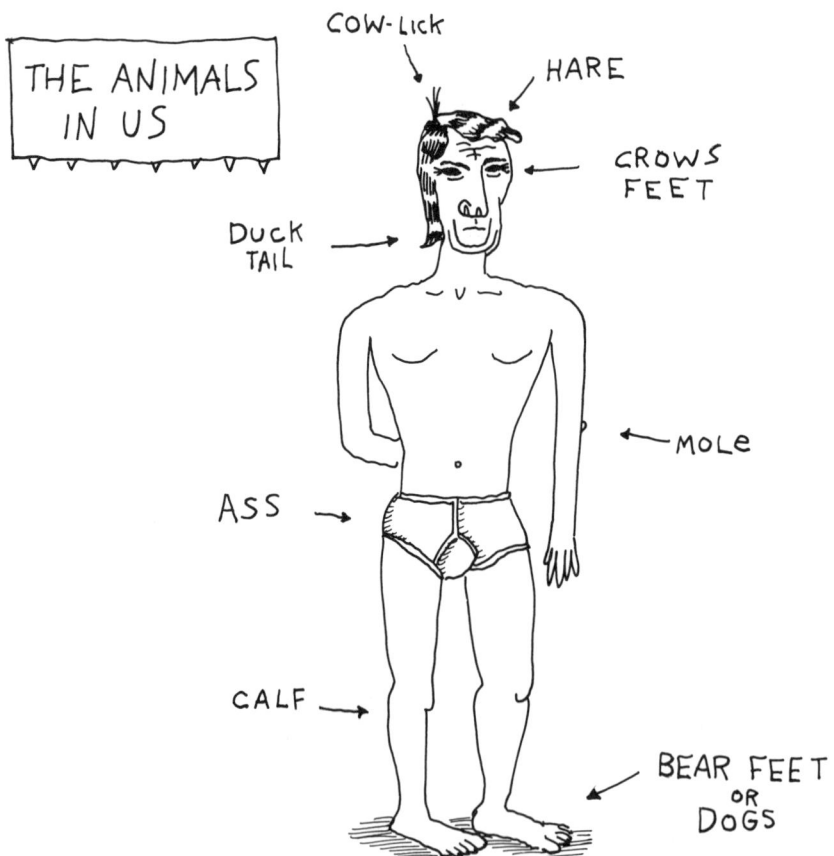

THE ANIMALS
IN US

COW-LICK

HARE

CROWS
FEET

DUCK
TAIL

MOLE

ASS

CALF

BEAR FEET
OR
DOGS

The day the
Earth burped.

on and on and on...

the birth of Radical Ant!

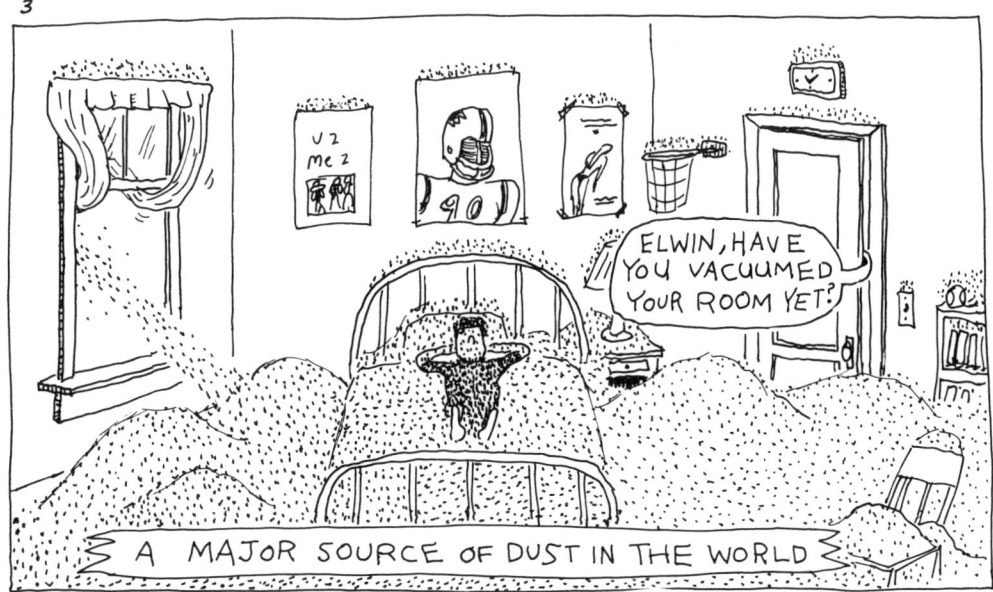

THE MOST FAMOUS RESIDENT OF THE BLACK LAGOON MAKES A MOMENTOUS DECISION.
THIS PLACE ISN'T FIT FOR MAN OR MONSTER!... I HEAR LOCH NESS IS NICE.

what's in a name?

EXXON VALDEZ

MEDITERRANEAN MOMA
(RENAMED)

Chernobyl

LENINS' PLAYGROUND
(RENAMED)

NO TRESPASSIN
LOVE CANAL

WHISPERING PINES
(RENAMED)

Three Mile Island

SEA BREEZE CONDOMINIMUMS
(RENAMED)

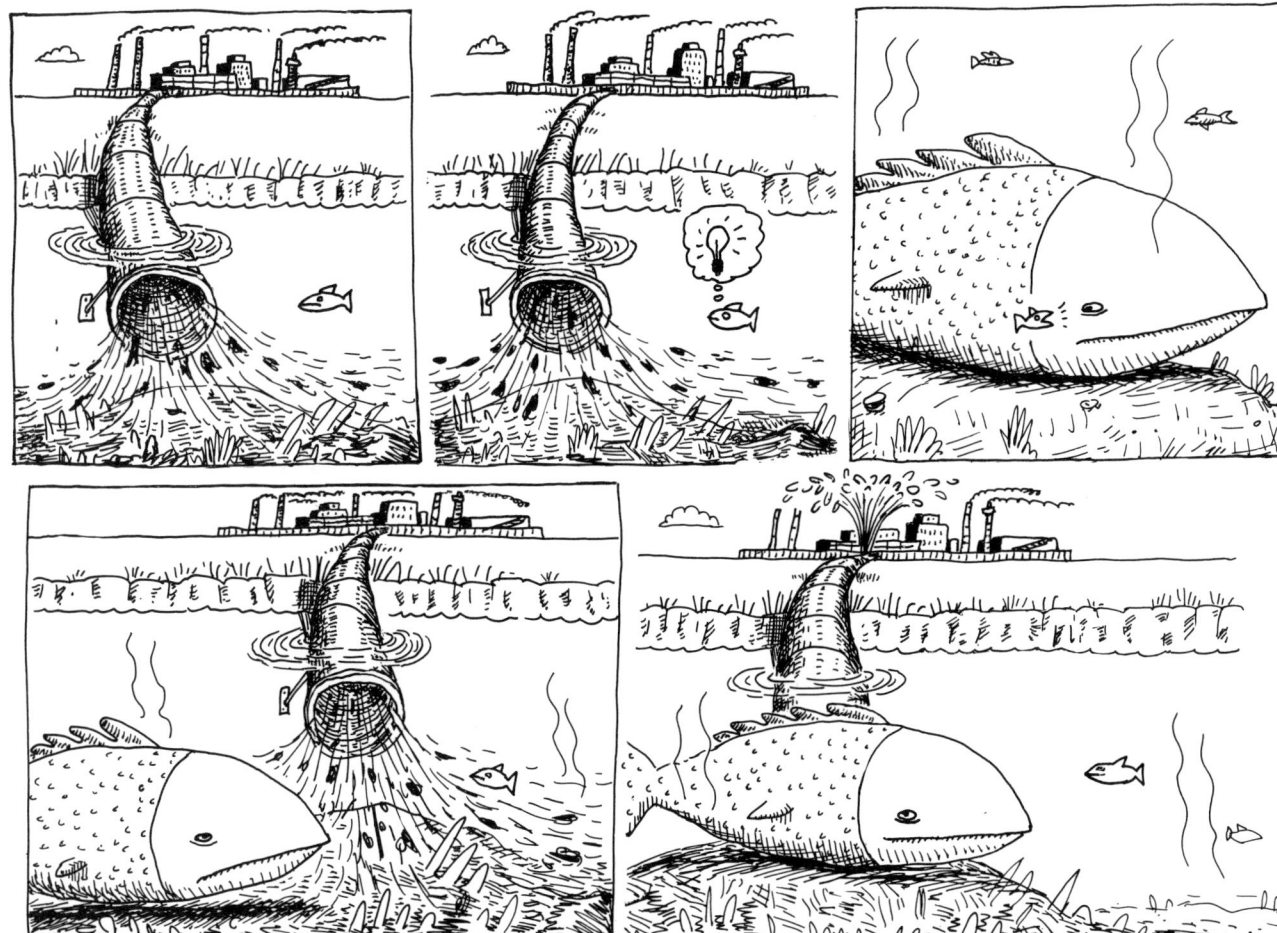

THE Army Corps of ENGINEER's Future Triumph's "PROGRESS TO CHOKE ON"

NIAGRA FALLS SPILLWAY

THE INTRODUCTION OF MOATS THROUGHOUT AMERICA.

THE WORLDS ONLY INTERSTATE
SYSTEM FOR BOATS.

THE GREAT ATLANTIC SEA WALL

The old fishing hole

The ole SWIMMING hole (RURAL)

THE OLD SWIMMING HOLE (City)

we hardly knew you.

KENNEDY   KING   MONROE   FIRMA

PARTLY SCATTERED NIGHT

"Interesting gravity we're having."

"Don't tell him I said so, but I think Dwayne's been in the toxic waste business a little too long."

·A MESSAGE TO ALL THIRD WORLD COUNTRIES·

FEEL LIKE YOUR'E STILL IN THE DARK AGES?

WELL don't JUST STAY there, MOVE UP!...

Before (WHAT A WASTE)

After (THIS CAN BE YOU)

...with a big dose of **PROGRESS.**

WHAT HAVE YOU GOT TO LOSE?

FOR MORE INFORMATION CALL OR WRITE TO THE INTERNATIONAL COUNCIL FOR PROGRESS TO CHOKE ON.

"I remember when all that used to be just cow pasture."

E Z Profit

AFTER STARTING MORE THAN 60 FIRES WITHOUT
A HITCH THIS ARSONIST'S LUCK FINALLY RUNS OUT.

MY MOM ALWAYS SAID I WAS OF SOUNDER BODY THAN MIND... SO IT WOULDN'T HAVE SURPRISED HER WHEN I DECIDED TO DIG THIS MYSTERIOUS HOLE.

HEINE

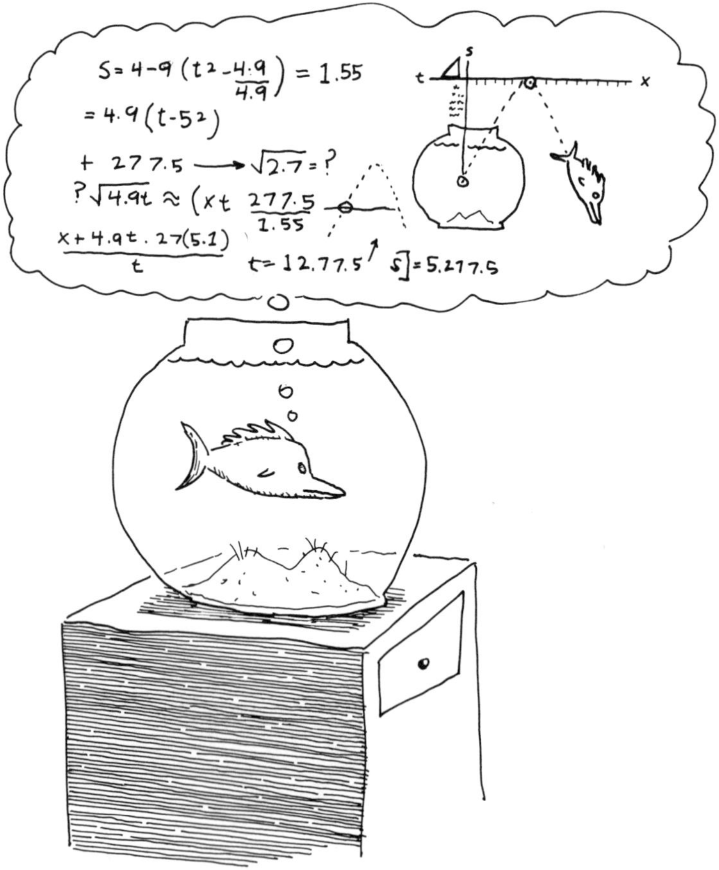

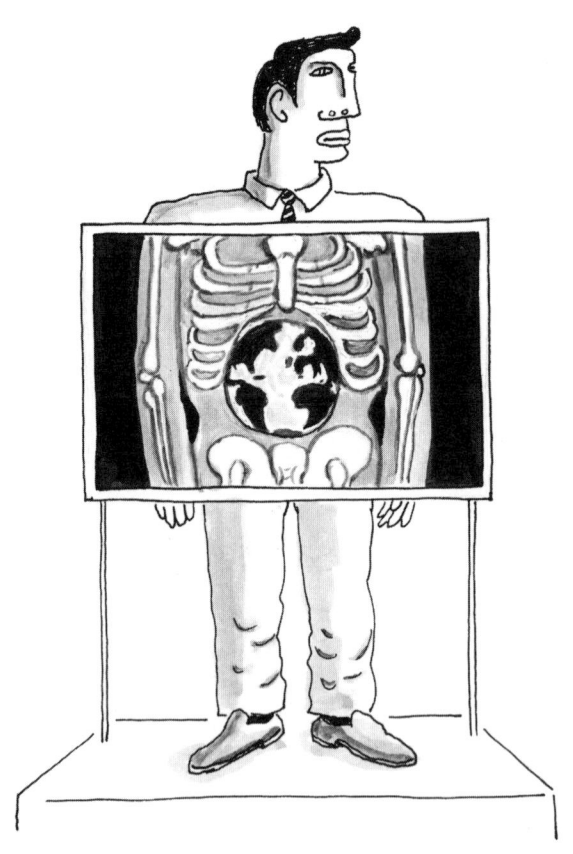

Wake up AND go back 2 Sleep Everybody

MANY OF THE EARTHS LAKES AND RIVERS ARE LITERALLY DISAPPEARING DUE TO THE EFFECTS OF SILTING.

EARLY STUDIES SHOW A NUMBER OF REGIONAL TOXIC WASTE DUMPS ARE LEAKING INTO NEARBY WATER-TABLES.

..THIS JUST IN A NEW REPORT SAYS THAT THE HOLE IN THE OZONE LAYER IS INCREASING AT AN ALARMING RATE.

AND THIS IS WHAT THE CROWDS LOOKED LIKE YESTERDAY AT AMERICA'S NEWEST FUN PARK SIX FLAGS OVER ELVIS.

TO MAKE YOUR VISIT AN ENJOY-ABLE ONE PLEASE LISTEN TO AND OBEY **ALL** PARK RULES.

BECAUSE OUR PARK IS SO POPULAR, TO HELP ALLEVIATE OVERCROWDING PLEASE LIMIT YOUR STAY TO NO MORE THAN 3 HOURS!

RULE # 4 ..ALL FIREARMS BROUGHT ONTO THE PREMISES MUST BE CHECKED & OKAYED AT THE N.R.A. INSPECTION CABIN.

LOOKS OK TO ME. ENJOY YOUR VISIT.

NEXT

INSPECTION

RULE # 9 ...TO BETTER APPRECIATE THE WILDERNESS EXPERIENCE PLEASE KEEP THE VOLUME DOWN ON YOUR TV's, RADIO's & COMPACT DISC's.

WHEEL OF FORTUNE

R RAA RRRR

RULE #11 ...WHEN HIKING THE NATURE TRAILS BEWARE OF FALLING TREES.

RULE #19 ..TO HELP SPEED THINGS UP WE ASK THAT ALL OUTDOOR COOKING BE DONE IN THE MICRO-WAVE OVENS LOCATED IN SPECIFIED AREAS THROUGHOUT THE PARK.

RULE #33 ,,IT GOES WITHOUT SAYING: GOLF CARTS ALWAYS HAVE THE RIGHT OF WAY.

RULE #47 ..ANY SWIMMING, SUNBATHING AND HIKING IN THE NUDE IS STRICTLY FORBIDDEN!

"You want those sodas in a "Organic Farmers Do It Better" glass.
a "I ♥ Dolphin Free Tuna Fish" cup or a "Have You Hugged A Tree Today" mug?"

HEINE

MOON OVER MIAMI

Other Cartoon Books from Menasha Ridge Press

A Mountain Bike Way of Knowledge *by William Nealy*

Kayaks to Hell *by William Nealy*

Whitewater Tales of Terror *by William Nealy*

Skiing Tales of Terror *by William Nealy*

Climbing Tales of Terror *by Tami Knight*

❍ *Menasha Ridge Press* ❍ *P.O. Box 43059* ❍ *Birmingham, Alabama* ❍ *35243* ❍